The Journey to Paradise

A unique and true story of an English family's association with Norway and it's people over a period of 50 years

by

Roger Stokes

2012

This book is dedicated to

Anne Helene Hanum

John Horder

and

My Mother

Without whom none of this
would have ever happened

First Published by Roger Stokes 2012

Copyright © 2012, Roger Stokes

ISBN

ROGER STOKES
Sunnybank
The Arch
Woodbury
Devon EX5 1LL
Tel: +44 (0)1395232350
http://www.woodburydevon.co.uk

Typesetting and layout by Roger Stokes

Printed and bound in Great Britain by Short Run Press Ltd.,
25 Bittern Road, Sowton Industrial Estate, Exeter, Devon EX2 7LW

CONTENTS

The Author and his wife in 2012

Introduction

This is a story that began in 1961 and continues until this day in 2012. So far it has encompassed four generations of our family over a period of 50 years. It is perhaps an unusual story with an even more unusual beginning!

We were then a local farming family from the village of Woodbury in the County of Devonshire, in the South West of England, and farming some 300 acres, of land. The family have been resident in the village continuously since 1537, although not always farming. My grandfather was a church bell hanger as was his father, and before that time family members had always taken up practical professions.

Throughout these pages I will be using the correct names of all the people involved, as a tribute to them. It is they who have really made the story, and I am just trying to document it. It is a unique story, and something which may never happen again, and I think should be logged in the annals of Norwegian history, in particular.

Sadly some of the forefathers of the story have now passed away, but at least six of the original individuals still survive in the country, in Hedmark and Oppland counties, and the city of Stavanger in Western Norway, and all have become great friends during this long period. The oldest, at the time of writing this story is now 93.

How did it start?

One day in 1961 my mother was paying in some money at our local bank at the nearby town of Exmouth. Whilst she was doing it, the cashier behind the counter asked her a question, quite out of the blue, which would change our lives far more that we could have ever imagined. What he said to her was, "Do you know a farming family who would take a Norwegian farmers son to work on the farm for the summer, so that he can learn some English?"

This was slightly different from the normal questions he would usually ask! My mother however immediately said "Yes, we will take him", without asking any other members of the family, and that is where this story begins. A story which has lasted now for 50 years!

The bank clerk from Exmouth was called John Horder, and had been known to us for many years, as back then a man seemed to have a job for life at one branch of the bank, instead of as today continually moved

on. Therefore we had a good rapport with him.

John Horder in 1961

Prior to asking my mother the question, John had been on a cycling tour of southern Norway, and on the way over on the ferry from England he had met a young Norwegian girl called Anne Helene Hanum, from Ilseng near Hamar. John was always a little eccentric, but a perfect gentleman, and he and Anne Helene got on well.

When the ferry docked at Oslo, Anne Helene, then only a teenager, was picked up by her farmer father Anders, who had driven down from Hamar specially to collect her. She was returning home after staying with a Welsh family for some time, so that she could learn some English. Later in the day while driving back up the E6, the car passed John Horder struggling on with his bicycle.

Recognised by Anne Helene, they stopped and offered him a lift as far as Hamar, and it was while they were chatting en route, that Anders said to him, "Do you know an English farmer who would take my son to work on the farm during the summer so that he could learn some English"? John said he would ask around when he returned home, and that is what he did. Luckily for our family, my mother was first in the line!

It was this one simple question, which at that point, unbeknown to all of us, would spark a long and enduring relationship between our two countries and their peoples for half a century to come.

Johan with his parents Anders and Ragnhild

What happened next

Johan Hanum was the first son to come to us in the summer of 1962, and he was with us for about a month. He came with a friend/cousin of his called Christian Ålstad, who lived near him in Norway. Christian had been fixed up also by John, to stay with another family called Murray, at Ottery St Mary, 5km from us, and who had a smallholding there. There was quite a bit of to-ing and fro-ing between the two places, but all had a good time.

At this time I was only about 19, and following a stay in hospital, had befriended a nurse who had been looking after me. Johan, being of similar age, also had an eye for the girls, and a few extra nurses were supplied for his visit. They had never seen a real Viking before and he had plenty of admirers. On one memorable occasion I remember that Johan, after a bit of fooling around, got himself stuck in a dustbin whilst on a visit to Dawlish Warren, a nearby beach area, and had to be extricated from it with some difficulty!

In the March of the following year, while winter was still very much in force, I took my first visit to the Hanum's. I remember arriving at Fornebu airport in Oslo on a BOAC Comet aircraft landing on a very icy runway. On touching down reverse thrust was given to the engines, which made everyone on board gasp, as it was not long after a Comet had crashed in the Mediterranean, and passengers were still a little apprehensive.

The train was taken to Hamar, where I was met by Anders and Johan. It was at this point that I found out that I was not now in England, and no one here spoke English very well. However, I soon learned that having a common interest in particular, reasonable communications could take place by using our joint imaginations and gestures!

Most of the snow had gone from around the farm, but there was still plenty up at Sjusjøen, where they had a cabin.

The Hanum family consisted of mother and father, Anders and Ragnhild, the two boys, Johan and Olav, and their two sisters Anne Helene and Sidsel. Sidsel of course, in 2012 is now one of Norway's best known and celebrated potters, and has been for some time.

Sidsel with her father in 1968

At this point of time when I met her first, she was only about 16 years old and still at school.

Of course I had never seen much snow in my life before, as in England it usually lasts only a couple of days. In Norway it was very different and took a little getting used to, to say the least! The next day, I was put to work in the potato shed where I had to help grade the potatoes into different sizes, at a temperature well below freezing, and this soon hardened me up quite quickly. However, the break for coffee was always eagerly looked forward to! In the evenings Anders would tell stories of what it was like around Hamar during the wartime, and how they used to

Sidsel showing Norwegian Foreign Minister Jonas Gahr Støre her designs at her exhibition in Lillehammer in 2010.

Photo by Ingunn Aagedal Schinstad

hide a radio deep inside a heap of potatoes, so that it wouldn't be found by the Germans if they came.

going down into a cellar below, and the hay and silage stored above to drop down to be fed to the cows. This I considered to be highly efficient. The farm

The Hanum farm barn in the 1960's

The Hanum farm was much smaller than ours in England, and very different. The cow house contained 20 – 30 cows which were kept in all the time, and fed zero grazed grass in the summer and silage during the long cold winters. I soon found out that Norwegian farm barns were designed extremely well to be able to accomodate the cows on one level with the muck

also had a large poultry department producing eggs housed within the same building, and this was basicly run by Ragnhild as her income.

After finishing the potato sorting, Anders decided that we should all go up to their cabin at Sjusjøen for the weekend to do some skiing. The cabin had originally been the top storey of one of their old barns, which some years before had been cut off from a barn and transported to the mountains and re-erected. It was a fine cabin and traditionally decorated inside. I of course had never seen anything like this before, and was really taken with it, and the memory of a Norwegian cabin was to remain with me for ever.

I had always said that one day I would like one myself, but at this point it was nothing more than a dream!

The family of course were excellent skiers, and had been brought up almost from birth to be able to ski. The morning after they arrived at the cabin they decided they would take me on a 20km round trip to Hornsjø and back, to see if I was up to it! I had only previously skied once before, on a trip to Switzerland when I was at school, but I soon remembered what I had to do.

We set off early in the morning after breakfast and followed in the ski tracks, which made life a bit easier. They really did not

The author, (left), with Anders, Johan and Ole Nashaug at the cabin in 1963

Taking a break on the Hornsjø trip

think I would make it, but I showed them that a young man from England could compete with the "Vikings" at their own game! We stopped at Hornsjø for coffee and then headed back again in time for supper. I have to admit that I found it difficult walk for a couple of days after, as my legs were so stiff. However, after getting my energy back I spent many an

A rest en route

Aprés ski

hour skiing in the beautiful area around the cabin. This was all before Sjusjøen was really on the map as a top grade ski centre as it is today.

On the ski tours I would often find myself skiing over large flat areas, which I thought was just ordinary ground underneath, but then I would find someone sitting beside a hole that they had drilled, and found out that I was skiing across a very large lake and was right in the middle of it! The holes of course were so that the people could go fishing through the ice. It is quite a clever system, as obviously under the ice it is very dark, but by drilling a hole in it, it lets the light in, and the fish come to the light and take the bait!

With this visit to Norway almost over, we returned back to the farm, and two days later I was back on the train to Oslo and heading home. This I thought might be the only visit I would ever make to the country that I had now fallen in love with.

How wrong I was to be!

The following year, Johan's brother Olav wanted to come to England and follow in the same pattern as his brother had done previously. He worked on our farm for the summer and learnt the English he wanted – plus a few words that he should not have! I went back again the following Easter, just a month before I was going to marry my lovely nurse who I was still in love with. She had previously been to Geilo in 1959 with a party of nurses, and following that also shared my love of the country.

I remember that on this visit I did some ploughing in a field at Hanum, which was a bit different to any ploughing that I had done at home. Having realised before that there was always a large heap of stones in the corner of most Norwegian fields, I now knew why they were there. I could hardly go 20 metres before the plough brought up yet another large stone or rock, bringing the tractor to a halt. Many days were also spent stone picking from the fields.

Life after the Hanum's

After getting married in 1964, we had a bit of a lull in our visits, but when our first child came along in 1965 we had a request from a cousin of the Hanum's if she could come and stay with us to also learn English. This young lady came from Lillehammer which was another 60km further up the E6, and she was was called Liv Blystad. Her father ran a large plumbing business in the town, but we had never met her before. She came over with her friend Berit Huuse, whose father was a shopkeeper in the Storgata there. Berit however, went to be with some people in London. In the end she didn't like it with the people she was with, and came down to Woodbury to stay with Liv and us. Liv came at a convenient time, and although she was not an "au pair", she spent a lot of time looking after our new baby boy called Simon, and pushing him around in his pram. Little did we know at the time, that 45 years later we would still be meeting Liv in the Gudbrandsdal almost every

From left to right standing: Liv, the author, Berit. Sitting: the authors wife Vera with baby Simon at Woodbury 1966

year. We have been good and solid friends ever since our first encounter.

opposite their cousins Anders and Ragnhild. We spent some time there over two winters, and

From left to right: Berit, Vera, Gerd and Gunnar Blystad

Following the initial visit of Liv, we returned to Lillehammer to stay with her parents, Gunnar and Gerd Blystad, at their house in the centre of the town in Mejdellsgata. This house is no longer there now, as it was demolished when the new hospital was built a few years later. From here it was possible to ski from the front door if you wanted, but the family also had a cabin at Sjusjøen, right

I remember having to slide down a snow covered slope to get to the cabin, as during the winter it had no direct access from the road due to the deep snow. Gunnar was a very wiry character, a bit like me, and had no problem traversing the slippery slope and getting out again, but I found it a little more difficult. Once inside the door I found it was very cold, as no heating is left on when the cabin is empty, but there was always a good supply of logs and when the big black stove in the corner was lit, the whole place warmed up in about half an hour. Water was the next problem as there was no running water to the cabin then, although I believe that there may have been a well underneath which always seemed to be frozen when I got there, so all water had to be brought in a churn from a hydrant about 100 metres away. Guess whose job it was to do that! Back in the late sixties and early seventies, none of the cabins at Sjusjøen had an inside toilet either, so if you needed to go during the night you had to dress up warmly, put your boots on and trudge out through the snow in your pyjamas in freezing temperatures. When you got there and opened the lid an awful smell came out. When you sat on the seat you almost stuck to it, as it was so cold. To an Englishman this was a little harsh!

I particularly remember one winter visit to Hanum in 1968, when foot and mouth disease in cattle was prevalent in England.

Anders was not sure if we should come, as we obviously came from an English farm, and he was very nervous about it. He feared that we would bring the disease to Norway which would destroy all the cattle in the country. Rather stupidly I told the authorities on arrival at Fornebu, that we were farmers, so on arrival we were whisked off to a clinic on the outskirts of Oslo somewhere, where we had to be decontaminated in some large cylindrical tanks, which I always thought resembled some of Hitler's gas chambers! Eventually extracting ourselves from these we caught the last train to Hamar in the evening. Of course our farm in England was 800km from the nearest outbreak of foot and mouth, but to get this point over to the Norwegian authorities was impossible. I made up my mind that if the same situation should happen again, I would say nothing. I wouldn't have come if there was any risk.

Following the unqualified success of our Norwegian liason, many more reciprocal trips followed in the years to come. Not only did we go on more trips there, but the senior members of the various families also spent time with each other.

My father and mother first went to stay with Anders and Ragnhild at Hanum, and later with Gunnar and Gerd Blystad in Lillehammer. In fact my father and mother made many trips during the 1970's, before my mother died in 1978. Father then went on trips alone for a while, and later with his cousin Betty, who had also been bereaved. Both Anders and Gunnar went out of their way to show them as much of Norway as possible, and they returned with stories of hairpin bends and mountain passes.

It was in 1968 that Anders and Ragnhild and their two daughters first came to visit us in Woodbury, and stayed with my parents as they had a larger house. However, that cemented a friendship that lasted for years after. They came here in the summer of that year, and during their stay, a serious rain storm caused much flooding in our village, which they were amazed to see. Water ran down the full width of the main street.

In 1974, because I had been awarded a Nuffield Farming Scholarship to study pigs in Eastern Europe, we had purchased a motor caravan to go on the trip. Having successfully completed that, in 1976 we

My parents (left) with Ragnhild Anders, Sidsel and cousin Olav Gjestvang visiting our farm in England in 1968

decided that perhaps a trip to Norway would be a good idea, so we set off from Harwich to the Hook of Holland by ferry, with two small children, and drove up through Holland, with Anders and Ragnhild at Hamar, and then at Mageli Camping near Tretten in the Gudbrandsdal. This particular area we really fell in love with, and always said that we would return one day. Once again, at the time this was just a dream, little knowing then what was likely to happen 27 years later! We ventured further up the country from there and toured around the Jotunheimen, wild camping at night in the wilderness of Norway. On the tops of the mountain areas there was still some snow in places, and we used to put our ice packs in the snow at night to keep them frozen. We also witnessed the pollution from mainland Europe, (we were told),

Hanum 1976 with Anders and Ragnhild and our children

Mageli Camping 1976

Germany, Denmark, and up the coast of Sweden to stay first which gave the snow pink and blue hues in places.

OL94 and beyond

Many visits to Norway took place during the following years, both by us and my parents, but in 1994 we decided to go to the Winter Olympics (OL94), which was held in Lillehammer. Everything for this was booked through an agency in England, and we had no idea where we would be staying, except that it would be with a family in Lillehammer. This was to be the start of yet another new adventure for us, as we had only been told their name and that they would meet us at Lillehammer station from the train. Their names were Terje and Alma Moe. Terje had just retired from being the headmaster of a local school, and Alma was an expert at handicrafts of many kinds. Both were extremely practical to say the least, and very friendly.

Having told Terje that I would be arriving at the train station wearing a yellow coloured anorak for easy recognition, we didn't realise that half the world would be arriving also wearing yellow coats! This caused some initial problems of recognition, but eventually when all the other coats had gone we were the only ones left, and Terje came up to us and said "You must be Roger and Vera I presume?" With our bags bundled into the car he took us on a slippery drive up to his house near the Maihaugen

Terje and Alma Moe

museum, where we were then welcomed by his wife Alma.

> Little did we know then that this would be the start of yet another great family friendship which would last for years to come.

Terje was a volunteer for OL, and had jobs to do during the two weeks we were there, mainly to keep the bobsleigh run at Hunderfossen tidy of all rubbish, a job he did very well, with others . Alma took us around the local Lillehammer area and showed us the best way to get to the Olympic Park by a footpath along from the top of the road above their house. This was quite a long walk, as was the walk into the town, both of which we traversed many times during the two weeks we were there, either during the day or late at night when we had returned from an event more distant. Both of them treated us far better than just the paying guests that we were, and in true Norwegian fashion welcomed us fully into their family structure.

We met their daughter Birgitte and her husband Tore Fossum, who had a small farm in Øyer, so we had something in common with them, and of course they spoke good English which was a bonus to us. Birgitte and Tore were part of a country dancing display at Hafjell during the games, and we have a long video of this.

Birgitte and Tore Fossum at OL94

More new friends being made by the "Man in the Yellow Coat" and his wife during OL94!

The weather was beautiful whilst we were there with blue skies all of the time, but the air temperature was not usually any warmer than -20°C. Although we thought we had come prepared for the cold, we had never experienced anything like this before, for such a long period. We found that because the bus transport was a bit overwhelmed in the early days, we had to wait in a bus queue for 4 hours before being able to get on board to go to Kvitfjell for the men's downhill, which had finished by the time we got there. To say we got a bit cold is an understatement! We attended both the opening and closing ceremonies, and the ski jumping, which were equally cold, plus other events in Hamar and Gjøvik, which were indoors and a bit warmer. Basicly we went to one event every other day, and on the "off" days did something different.

On one day we took the train down to Oslo, and then on to Moss, where Vera my wife wanted to go to attend a dog show.

Vera had been a breeder of Miniature Dachshunds for a number of years, and was attracted by an advertisment for a Dachshund show there. It was a bit further than we thought with the final bit having to be done by taxi, but we got there and were made very welcome.

On another day off we took the train again to Hamar to visit Anders and Ragnhild who we hadn't seen for a couple of years. Here we met up again with Anne Helene and her husband Jarle. We had not seen Anne Helene for several years, maybe only once since her visit to Woodbury in the 1960's, as she had moved away to make her home in Stavanger where her husband had his job.

Anne Helene, (the girl from the ferry), and her husband Jarle during the Olympic period

For us, we thought that attending these games would be the pinnacle of our years visiting this wonderful country, and despite OL94 being described as "The best winter games ever!", which it really was, little did we know what was still in store for us in the future.

The immediate future was quick to come, as when we arrived back at Fornebu to take the plane back to England, we had checked in our baggage and sent it off down the belt to the loading bay, or so we thought. Due to the games, security had been tightened, and a large customs lady approached us within minutes and said, "Please come with me". One of our suitcases had been pulled from the belt, and was apparently causing some serious concern with the authorities. "Please open it up", said the lady very sternly. When opened, it was clear to us what had caused the problem. Vera, my wife was very keen on Norwegian handicrafts, and whilst at Lillehammer had bought some wooden tuplips and spoons, and also some tubes of paint, to paint them with when she got home. There were six or eight of these tubes, and unfortunately she had bundled them together and put an elastic band around them, to stop them going everywhere in the case. To an X Ray machine they had looked like sticks of explosives which could make a big bang! We all had a bit of a laugh, and re packed the case, and all was well. However, it was good to see that the system really worked if required.

This reminds me of a previous incident some fourteen years before, when I was returning back again to England with our young son Simon, who I had brought over to do some skiing at Sjusjøen. We had taken the train back to Oslo, and had gone to the SAS Hotel to wait for a bus to take us to the airport. During the week we had been looking at the television news most evenings, and were aware that Walter Mondale, who was then the US Vice President, had been visiting Norway that week to trace his ancestors. This was at a time of considerable

East – West tension. We arrived quite early in the morning at the hotel, and initially were the only two people sitting there waiting for the bus. It soon became apparent that the area had been cleared by the US security men who were accompanying Mondale, as he was soon to be arriving and they didn't want any trouble. Of course we knew nothing about this and sat there quite innocently, but we were aware that we were being "watched" quite closely. When we looked around, the room was totally staked out by men with a cable coming from their ear, and an obvious hand gun in a readily available position, so I told Simon not to make any sudden moves. We all sat looking at each other for over an hour, and it was quite a stand off, but I was absolutely convinced that if we had stood up quickly, or moved suddenly, we would have been shot first with the questions being asked later – not the other way around!

The beautiful Gudbrandsdal Valley

23

However, following our earlier travels in eastern Europe, we had become accustomed to problems crossing borders, with men with guns, and took this in our stride and had a bit of a laugh about it later.

Not easily put off by minor hiccoughs, the following winter we returned again to Lillehammer for the games "Re-union", but had decided to stay in a hotel in the town this time. Hoping to remain incognito for this visit, we soon found out that this was not possible due to the highly efficient bush telegraph system which appears to exist in Norway. Being such a low populated country, and divided up in to long valleys, we soon found out that more or less everyone within a certain community knew everyone else and what was going on. It would be no good trying to be a spy there, because you would stand out like a sore thumb! We later found out that almost everyone in the Gudbrandsdalen valley knows, or knows of, almost everyone else, because they probably went to a central

school together, even if they are 50km apart. In England this is quite the opposite. In the event, we were having a rest on our bed in the hotel one afternoon and there was a loud knock on the door which woke us up. We opened the door to find Alma standing there who said, "Why aren't you staying with us?" From our point of view, we had not wanted to over do our welcome from the year before, which had been so good, but the following year we were back again at Alma's!

Two years later in 1998 we decided to take a summer tour from England to the North Cape with our own car from home. To do this we had first to drive to Newcastle some 8 hours drive from Woodbury, to take the ferry across to Bergen. The trip of 24 hours on the ferry was awful with very rough seas, and I was confined to bunk all the way with extreme sea sickness. Even the Captain had to come and see if I was still alive! I vowed never to do this again, but shortly after, the ferry service ceased anyway.

This also turned out to be the journey of a lifetime, and we had allowed three weeks to complete the trip.

On leaving Bergen we travelled through Voss and cross country following the road between Sognefjell and the Jotunheimen which we had travelled in 1976 with the motor caravan, to Otta. Stopping just north of Otta for the night we headed on again the next day and got to Steinkjer where we stayed for the second night. On again up the E6, which is the main highway from bottom to top of the country, we arrived at a lovely caravan park just a few kilometers below the Arctic Circle at Krokstrand where we took a cabin to break the journey. There were still three more days of driving ahead before we would be able to cross over to Magerøya, the island on which the North Cape or Nordkapp is situated. After a ferry crossing,we finally arrived in Honningsvåg in the early afternoon in a torrential rainstorm, and drove on to find somewhere to stay. It was good to get there, but if we were to see the midnight sun we would

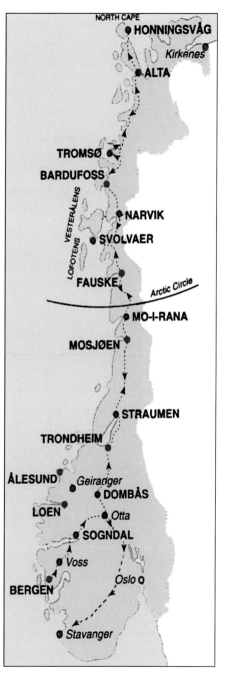

only be able to have a short rest, and then drive the last few kilometers to Nordkapp itself.

Unfortunately we had not picked the best of evenings to go there as the cloud cover was almost 100%, but after a long wait with hundreds of other people of all nationalities, a gap appeared in the clouds which let us glimpse the sun. Back again we drove to our hotel without any lights on the car at 2 am in the morning. We had never witnessed 24 hour daylight before, and it was quite incredable. We went up again during the next day to take a better look at the surrounding area, and saw many reindeer in the wild, plus snow in some of the hollows which had not melted since the winter. It is indeed a bleak place at any time of the year.

Before I had left England I had an unfortunate incident with a hammer, and had hit my thumb with it. The nail had gone very black and was

obviously going to come off at some stage. As it happened this took place at Nordkapp, which really was quite a fitting moment. I could not allow myself just to throw part of my body away to blow in the wind, so I held a small ceremony and dug a hole and buried it near the statue of the lady. Hopefully it is still there to this day, and perhaps I will go back sometime

The statue of two ladies at Nordkapp!

26

The ultimate holiday snap - the top of the World - well nearly!

and retrieve it. I may be the only person in the world to have my DNA in two countries at the same time - who knows!

> If nothing else, I consider it was at that point that I staked my claim to a part of Norway, something I had always wanted to do!

It took us another week to return as far as Lillehammer, back down the same E6, as there is no alternative. Here, 30km above Lillehammer we stayed once again at Mageli Camping, where we had stayed previously 22 years before. We occupied one of their timber cabins for a couple of days, so that we could visit our locally based Norwegian friends in and around Lillehammer. We became quite friendly with Tor Mageli, the owner of the park, and returned, (by air), for several of the following years. We would tell Tor that we would be a little late arriving and he would leave the cabin key in a place that we could find it, to let ourselves in.

On leaving Mageli, we took the road past Lillehammer and on to

Mageli Camping 1976

Gjøvik, and went cross country again through Rjukan, where we stayed for the night, and then on to Hovden. From here we followed the big roads and the small roads back to Stavanger, from where we took the boat back to England.

On one of our subsequent visits to Mageli we started looking in the windows of estate agents, to see if there were any cabins that we could buy in the area, and to get an idea of sizes and prices. Eventually, when sat at home using my computer one evening and surfing agents websites, I came across one or two potential properties which looked interesting. However, they were all a bit run down, and would need some work done on them.

During our next visit we went to look at those that we had on the short list, and also some that were very much more expensive. The latter were soon ruled out, as being outside our financial capabilities. One of the others on the list was very nice, but too large a property for us to be able to maintain from England, and it was in the wrong place to be able to get out of unaided in the winter snows. This left us with only one possible contender aptly called Lykkebo – translated in to English meaning "Lucky House".

For us this seemed to be our own stroke of luck, and after viewing it from the outside decided to pursue it further. It appeared from the brochure that it had been on the market for some time. The next day we were shown around by the agent, and were left to contemplate what to do. The price was still a little too high in view of some of the work which would have to be done on it. We returned to England still pondering what to do, but had fallen in love with it. The view out of the front window across the lake Losna was out of this world for an Englishman, and you could even still see Mageli in the distance.

Many negotiations took place via fax and email to the agents, and a price was eventually agreed with the sellers, who would also do some of the

The stunning view from the front window

repairs required before we took it over. However, before anything could be finalised, we found out that we would have to get a 'D' number. That is a Norwegian National Insurance number, before the deal could be transacted. Everything in Norway appears to revolve around this number. We also had to get a bank account to be able to pay local bills like electric, insurance and council charges. Luckily, our long time friend Liv was then working at the bank at Segalstad Bru, so we went there and had our photos taken, and filled in the necessary forms to set up an account. All was now complete to be able to conclude the transaction, so I went to our bank here at home, where John Horder had worked some 40 years before, and the money was transferred across.

The cabin viewed from the mountainside

Lykkebo – a new beginning

Eventually, on the 5th August 2003 it became ours, and my long term dream of having a cabin in Norway had at last become a reality. We were now the proud owners of 800 square metres of this wonderful country, plus a cabin to live in when we were here. The previous owners, whose family had built it, came to hand over the keys, which is customary in Norway, and show us how to operate the things inside. We were extremely lucky that they had left virtually everything inside the cabin for us, so we were able to move in without having to go out and furnish it or buy anything to get started. However, the next morning we woke up and wondered just what we had done, and if it had really been the right decision! Since that one moment of doubt, we have never had any regrets.

From our early days of the 1960's at Sjusjøen, this old cabin was a luxury, as it had both a toilet inside, water to the cabin through a pipe from a well across the road, and mains electricity. It even had an electric water pump. No more plodding out in the night in freezing conditions or fetching water, although there were one or two things that still needed doing. These however could wait until the next year.

Ole and Lisbeth

The next day we introduced ourselves to Ole and Lisbeth, who were our neighbours and lived in the small farm about 100 metres away. We had met Ole briefly before, when we came to view the cabin a few months earlier. We seemed to get on quite well at this meeting, and soon realised that we had to depend quite a lot on both of them for local information, such as where to get different things etc. Over the following years our friendships have strengthened, and Ole has now visited us twice in England. We had a quiet week here following the take over, and bought a few small things for the cabin, and then we returned home to England. Three months later in October, we returned to do a few more major jobs!

anyway, so looked at various other local properties to see what would be the best colour to repaint it. House colours in Norway are fairly basic, red, yellow, blue, green, or black or white, but here they were always traditional colours. We decided to go for the Gammel Rød, (old

Lykkebo when we viewed it the first time - in need of a bit of tender loving care

When we bought the cabin it was painted a very faded blue-green colour, which certainly needed refreshing. We didn't really like the colour

red), which seemed to be the predominant colour in the area, so a trip to Karlsen Fargehandel at Segalstad Bru found us the proud possessors of 20 litres of

32

suitable paint, brushes and a ladder. It took four days of hard work by both of us to paint all round with the red, one side each day. Then some white had to be applied to the windows which was a little more difficult as the timber was very narrow between the glass. In the end however we considered that we has improved the look of the place considerably, and all the hard work had been worth it. As the cabin was in an area where

The new Lykkebo

there are many footpaths, we would intersperse working with walking, to make a bit of a change. At the end of our time there on this visit we had to put the cabin "to bed" for the winter, and make sure all the water was drained out of the pipes to stop them freezing, something we would do many times thereafter.

On some of the visits to Norway I came on my own, and the first of these was in January 2004.

This was the first time that I had driven on the roads in winter. All went very well for the first 130km, until the last 200 metres, when a lapse in my concentration allowed the car to veer slightly to the right, and the front wheel caught the snow on the edge of the driveway to the cabin. This pulled the car to one side and into a small ditch before I realised what was happening. Luckily the car was not damaged but just stuck underneath on the snow. There was no way out without a pull! I went to find Ole, but he couldn't be found, as he was somewhere in the forest cutting some timber. I went to the neighbouring farm, whose son offered to tow me out with his tractor, which only took a few seconds. Since then I have had a far greater respect for the conditions on winter roads!

country areas during the winter, and our short walks up and down the local roads caused a bit of consternation. I think we went under the heading of "Mad Englishmen!" However, it is a good time to visit friends, and I went to Øyer to see Terje and Alma in their new retirement flat. They had moved from Lillehammer the year before.

The winter roads have to be cleared with a snowblower and can have hidden suprises!

In May of the same year, on the way up from Gardermoen, I stopped off at Hamar to see Raghnild at Hanum. She was very pleased to see me and gave me a big hug. I had not seen her for 10 years since OL94, and of course she was now 10 years older. Unfortunately Anders had died a few years before and he was sadly missed by all of us.

During the winter period you soon learn that you cannot do very much outside, as it is too cold, and the snow is usually too deep. Compared with England, you hardly ever see a Norwegian walking outside in

He was one of the stalwarts of the early days, and a man with a very good sense of humour.

The patio

When we bought the cabin there was one thing missing, and that was a patio. The door in to the cabin from it, had been built into the original design, but the patio had never been constructed. The door itself was some 60cm above the outside ground level, and wasn't used for this reason. It was on this visit that I decided something needed to be done about it, and I started sizing up the options. I measured up and drew a plan, and consulted Ole about the size of the timbers neccessary to take the winter snow load, when it slipped off the roof, with the view that on our next visit in July I would construct it myself.

I went back to England and thought a bit more about it, and decided it was definately the right thing to do, so both of us returned on the 23rd June geared up with all the tools that were

The door to the area for the patio was too high to be used

up all the timber that would be needed, and the following day it was delivered by lorry. It was unloaded with a mechanical hoist, but we had to carry each piece across the small access bridge and stacked it up beside the cabin. Our work could now begin.

required to build a patio. A heavy duty electric drill to make the fixing holes in the concrete base, hammers, spanners, bolts and all. Our suitcases were very heavy!

On the way up from Gardermoen Vera drove the car for a while, as she had never driven on the right before, and I thought she should try to get used to it in case anything happened to me. She got on very well, but was glad to hand the driving back to me!

The next morning I went down to the Samverkilag, (Co-op), at Tretten and ordered

First we had to fix some boards to the base wall of the cabin and get them level. This was obviously very important. Ole would come and inspect at various intervals to see if I was doing the job correctly. I don't think he was sure that an Englishman he had not known for very long, could undertake such a project, however all the

ourselves, and the patio door was used for the first time. The other advantage was that it gave us an awful lot more room to move about, which was great, rather than just sitting inside all the time and looking out of the window.

way through his advice was taken on board by me and was very useful.

By the 3rd July the floorboards were laid in place, and Liv and her husband Erik came and took coffee with us, balancing on the loose boards. Ole was consulted later about how wide the gap should be between the boards. "Not so wide that your money falls down between!", he said. After working out a good average, as I didn't want to get to the other side and find I had a large gap or a small gap, over 1000 screws were used to fix the boards down. Thank goodness for the electric screwdriver! It was good then, as we could now sit outside in the fresh air and sun and have a cup of coffee

After the floor was fixed, a boundary fence was erected around the whole patio, and some steps constructed to go down to the front, plus a couple of gates to keep the wild animals from having a party there when we were back in England! With the small amount of timber that was left over I made a table, which has been very useful throughout all our time there.

We could now sit and enjoy our coffee!

So what else have we done

Despite the fact that it might seem that we are working all the time, we did have a few days off, and on one Saturday in July met up with Terje and Alma Moe, who with their daughter Birgitte and husband Tore, took us to their seter up over the top at Åstdalsætra. This was a most amazing experience, as previously seters were things we only learnt about when we were at school in England. Everything was explained to us as to how the system worked, and that virtually every local farm had it's own seter. Some were many miles from the home farm, usually on high ground, where the farm animals would go for their summer holidays for a couple of months. Whilst there we saw moose in the distance and reindeer on the way back. The back roads to these seters are usually only hardcored roads, and very dusty in the summer time, and any vehicle you are in, comes back

Birgitte explaining the seter system at Åstdalsætra

39

extremely dirty. These roads also contain a lot of potholes, and a lot of driving expertise has to be used to try to avoid them, otherwise you have a very bumpy ride!

Seters all have living accomodation on the premises, where the farmer and his family can live as well during the summer. These places are inaccessable during the winters, and usually buried under one to two metres or more of snow. However, these areas are what I call "Real Norway". We consider ourselves to have been very privileged to have been taken to such places, as they are not on what might be called the normal tourist route.

One evening we were invited to go on an organised walk with the Tretten History Society, and our neighbour Lisbeth decided that she would take us in her car. This was most interesting, and we went from Kråbølstuga to Svartvåtner , and on the way we were told about the wartime

On the History Society walk to Svartvåtner

40

exploits that had happened there with the English soldiers. The book, "The Naked Soldiers", was written by an English man after the last war, and is based in the Gudbrandsdal Valley. It recalls how British soldiers were sent to Norway to repel the Germans, but how their equipment and ammunition was torpedoed as they entered the coastal fjords, and they were largely left to fend for themselves - hence the name "The Naked Soldiers" Luckily Brit-Ida Berg Hansen, who had invited us via the Moes, came along and acted as interpreter, which really made the evening go well. There is a lot of history around the hill sides of Tretten.

Many of our summer evenings have been taken up with walking around Musdalseter, Skeikampen, and the Moksa Dam areas, which are local to us, and where there are many different walk paths that can be taken, and a lot of old buildings to be seen. Compared with where we live in England, everywhere in Norway away from the main roads, is so very quiet and peaceful.

During our walk with the History Society we were chatting to Brit-Ida about how we came to be so fond of Norway, and she said her daughter Camilla was a reporter with the local newspaper Gudbrandsdølen Dagningen, (GD), and that our story would make an interesting article for her – would we be willing to talk to her? At the time the paper was doing a weekly series on people's ideas of "Paradise". Perhaps rather foolishly we said "Yes"! At 7.30am next morning there was a knock on the cabin door, and Ole was there in his pyjamas holding a mobile phone in his hand, saying that he had a reporter on the line and would it be OK if she came in half an hour to interview us! Not wishing to let Brit-Ida down we agreed and hurriedly got ourselves dressed. Camilla duly arrived, complete with photographer Torbjørn Olsen, and on the 13th July we had a two page spread in GD, much to our surprise. This triggered off a lot of local interest, and several cars were observed trying to find out just where this mad English couple lived. The next

- Tretten er vårt

paradis

Ekteparet Vera og Roger Stokes fra England er så forelsket i Tretten at de like godt har kjøpt seg hytte der.

Ekteparet Vera og Roger Stokes ble så forelsket i Tretten og Gudbrandsdalen at de kjøpte hytte i Musdalen.

Av Camilla Berg Hansen

TRETTEN: Kjører du lenge nok på en kronglete grusvei langt oppe i Musdalen, kommer du til et punkt hvor hele dalen åpner seg foran øynene dine og Losna langt der nede speiler himmelen og liene opp mot deg så du ser all

Engelsk ektepar fant lykken i Musdalen

herligheten dobbelt. Der, på en selvsnekret veranda, sitter et engelsk ektepar og drikker kaffe av kopper med stråmønster, og nyter synet av sitt favorittsted på jorda: Tretten.

Utsikt

- Det er så utrolig vakkert her på Tretten, er det ikke?, sier Vera Stokes og ser utover bygda hun er så glad i.

Utsikten gjorde utslaget da hun og mannen Roger var på leting etter hytte på Tretten.

- Om vinteren sitter jeg her

om kvelden og ser utover lie Det er så vakkert når det lyse vinduene på alle gårdene og l sene borti der, peker Roger.

For dem som har vært på T ten ei vinternatt før, er det k skje litt uforståelig at et ekte fra landsbyen Woodbury nær I mouth sørvest i England k være så til de grader fascinert bygda. En forklaring må til.

Roger kan fortelle at han h feriert i Norge siden 1963. Fa lien hans var kjent med en fa lie på Hamar, og slik ble h kjent med landet vårt. Siden (gang har han besøkt Norge o

ngt oppi lia på Tretten, har ekteparet Vera og Roger Stokes fra England funnet sitt lykkebo. *(FOTO: TORB*

time we went to the shops we had to wear dark glasses for fear of being recognised!

When we had been staying with Terje and Alma for OL94, they took us out to lunch one Sunday at Glomstad, just above Tretten. This is a wonderful place for good traditional Norwegian food, plus a fantastic view up the Losna, and was a place that we had never forgotten. We have now been there many times since on our own, and we always take our English visitors there if they come to stay with us. Janna Glomstad is a wonderful lady who really knows how to put on a good selection of Norwegian food.

One thing which is different from home is the fact that many of the farm animals that roam the forests in the summer, are fitted with a bell so that they can be located. This gives lovely background music to the whole area, and is far better than the motor cars and large lorries that we get at home. If something should startle the animals, they all rush up the field and all the bells ring together, sounding like "ding dong merrily on high"!

nger. Han og kona Vera
te å reise rundt i cam-
l sammen, og i 1976 fant
i for godt å legge seg inn
geli Camping på Tretten.
ar det gjort: En livslang
se blomstret.
et er så fredelig og rolig
fære her, sier Vera, og
rer at hun og Roger
ter fra en veldig hektisk
mende landsby.
ger forteller at paret likt
første dag på Mageli.
et er så fint å sitte der og
vakre Losna som glitrer i
ola skinner alltid på Ma-
nes han.

.ebo

nettet fant paret fram til
tte som de kjøpte i fjor.
ette heter plassen «Lyk-

- Her vil vi bare nyte livet.
Vi skal ta med alle fem barne-
barna våre hit. De er glade i å
gå tur i fjellet, akkurat som oss,
og vi har lyst til å ta dem med
ut på ski, sier Vera.
Bortsett fra fjellturer, er
Roger veldig interessert i lo-
kalhistorie. Han har skrevet en
bok om landsbyen sin i England, og nå liker han å høre
mer om Tretten.
- Jeg har fått en bok om sol-
dater i området her under an-
dre verdenskrig, sier han, og
viser fram sitt eksemplar av
«The Naked Soldier». Men
Roger er ikke nødt til å lese
bøker på engelsk. Gjennom
årenes løp har han lært seg å
snakke, derimot, synes han er
veldig vanskelig. Likevel skulle
man tro han har anlegg for å
lære det, for han har allerede

en utpreget norsk ak:
engelsken sin, den e
mannen.
- Kanskje det, ler ha
- Jeg har jo mange
venner. Folk er veldig l
ge og hjelpsomme h
han, og legger til at ha
leter etter et godt no
hjemme i England.
Vera bærer også et li
ke Norge med seg til h
det. Hun har hengt op
fra hytta og bygda på
net sitt i Woodbury. Fo
er det ingen tvil.
- Hvis du lukker øy
tenker at du er på det v
stedet du kan forestil
hvor er du da?
- Her, selvsagt!, er c
tante svaret.

43

All the sheep have a bell around their necks and make fine music!

When we bought the cabin, there were still one or two unfinished matters inside. The fireplace had no stone top to it, and the electric water pump position beside the fireplace had no door to it. These had been bugging us for some time, so finding that there was a stone factory in Tretten, we went to see them to see what might be possible. With the measurements supplied by us, they cut out a top and we took it back in the rear of the car. It was quite long and weighed 55kg., so Ole's help was required to help us get it into place. Whilst talking to the man at the stone factory I asked him if he had ever been to England, and he said that his daughter had been at a language school at Sidmouth, which is a small seaside town only 15km from where we live. What a small world it is!

That finished the fireplace to satisfaction, and I found an old door in the wood shed which I cut down to fit the size of the opening in front of the pump. When fixed in place, the whole fireplace looked much better, and the pump was a lot quieter when operating. As this was the last visit before the winter, and we were going home the next day, the water system had to be once again drained down so that there was no chance of it freezing.

44

The finished fireplace with new stone top and door

Our daughter Helen was the first of our family to visit the cabin in January 2005, and when we arrived we found that the snow had slipped off the roof and fallen onto the path to the wood shed. This made it impossible to get to the shed to get to the logs, so we had to clear a way through about a metre and a half depth of snow before we could light the stove and get warmed up. Ever since then I have always left enough logs inside the cabin to last for at least one day, which would give us some time to sort out any problems, and be warm at the same time.

We then noticed that when the snow had slipped, it had also bent the guttering and that had to be repaired before we came home again. Our friend Liv had told us before, that if you have a cabin there is always something to do, and this appears very true. However this was not a problem for us, as we always liked to be doing something, but found it

Repairs are something that you have to do all the time - winter or summer

into the tracks and moved off. Down the slope we went until we heard a loud scream coming from the other direction. There was an almighty collision with some others who were coming the other way, and we all tipped over in the snow. What we hadn't realised was that it was a clockwise circuit and we were going anticlockwise.

was always better to do it in the summer when it was warmer!

Helen took some ski lessons at Skeikampen for two or three days, as she had not skied before, and by the end of the week was reasonably proficient. When going to Skei we had noticed a shooting range not far away which was illuminated in the evenings, with a nice machined ski track around it where the youngsters trained for the biathlon. One evening, she and I took our skis there and thought that we would do a circuit, not realising that it was practice night for the young biathletes. Skis attached, we got

They politely informed us that we were bad people! - but we all had a good laugh, and then carried on in the correct direction!

The next evening I filled up the stove with logs, so that it would go for some time without refilling, and closed the draught hole. Half an hour later there was an enormous bang, and there was smoke everywhere. All the smoke alarms went off which made an awful noise, and we could hardly see where to go, so we opened all doors so that the smoke could go out. What I should have done of course was not to close the draught hole completely, and leave it a little open, so that air could flow through. There had been a build up of gases inside the stove to the point where the logs ignited, which also ignited the gases, and then bang. We have learned a lot of things by experience, and this was one of them!

that with all the trees that there are in Norway, logs would be cheap to buy, but as it happens, they are probably the most expensive in the world! Ole was consulted, and he talked to a neighbouring farmer who owned the forest area behind us. This

This is one of the major parts of a cabin owners duties each year

When we bought the cabin, it came with a shed full of logs. It soon became apparent that the shed was fast becoming empty, and some thought had to be given as to where we could get some more. You would think

farmer kindly said that we could go into his forest and cut up any trees that had fallen down, of which there were many. So, armed with a chain saw supplied by Ole, I set off into the woods to see what I could do. This was not an easy task, as most Norwegian forests are not on level ground, but on a slope of at least 45° or more. This made standing up safely very difficult with a chain saw in your hands. The other factor was that where the trees were, was a long way from the path way where they had to be taken to be loaded

More hard work to split all the new logs!

for transportation back to the cabin. So, cutting trees and carrying logs at 45° is not for the faint hearted! Anyway, a pile of logs was made at the nearest point in the path, and the chainsaw, fuel can, and oil can

carried back to the farm up a very steep slope by hand. Ole had previously offered me the use of his tractor with box on the back, to go and pick then up, so I drove down this time which was easier.

Heavily laden, I arrived back at the cabin and tipped the box outside, after which all the logs had to be m a n h a n d l e d again into a wheel barrow to the wood shed. The larger ones had to be split with the aid of an axe into four

A winters supply, which has to dry for 12 months

or six pieces so that they would fit into the stove. I can quite see why logs do cost so much to buy as there is a lot of work involved, which is not appreciated at first glance. However, all was worth it, as the shed had now been filled up again. This is a process that has been undertaken every year since then.

During our travels in Norway we had always noticed that most dwellings had a flag pole, where the national flag would be raised on special days, or at half mast for a death in the family. Not wishing that we were going to die, I asked Ole, "Where could I get a flagpole?" "Leave it to me", he said, "I will find something by the next time you come".

On arriving back again in June of that year, two trees were lined up by Ole's saw bench. "Which one would you like?", he asked. I said, "I will have that one, that is the straightest", pointing to the best of them. He then said that I would have to remove the bark so that the tree could dry out, and that I must not paint it for twelve months. Using a spoke-shave that he loaned me, I spent the next hour or two removing bark.

Now I had to think about where I was going to erect the flagpole. Eventually I found a place which I thought would be

Two candidates for flagpole

49

suitable, by doing a bit of prodding of the ground. Unfortunately most Norwegian land has a large underground content of rock, which is not always visible, through which it is impossible to dig. Thinking that my chosen spot was OK, I started to dig with my iron bar and shovel, and I was lucky. I went down a metre without a problem, found some pieces of 6"x 2" which had been left over from the patio construction, and inserted them into the hole to make a swivel base for the eventual pole next year.

One thing I forgot to mention earlier was the fact that apart from the cabin having an inside WC, where did all the water go when it was flushed? Everything drains into a sealed tank about 15 metres away from the cabin, but when it is full it has to be emptied, and it became full! The man with the lorry, "Oppland Miljøteknikk", were telephoned, and they came to suck it out, which they have done every year since.

When the tank is full it must be emptied, or we have problems!

Team Stokes! Three generations of the family skiing at Skeikampen

In February 2006, our son Simon, (the one who was the baby in the earlier picture!), and his wife Nicola, and their three boys Ben, Tom and Wills came with us. This was to be the boy's first attempt at skiing, and they were very keen to try it. Like Helen previously, they also went to Skei and had several days of lessons, and by the end of the week had become very proficient. We were quite amazed by their progress in such a short time, and at the end of the week, Wills, the youngest, who seemed fearless, skied from the top to the bottom of Skeikampen mountain on his own, without any ski sticks!

During the time they were there, we took them on a tour of the area, to Hafjell, to Hunderfossen to see the Bobsleigh run, and in to Lillehammer to go shopping, but they couldn't wait to get back on the ski's. However, they had to go home a couple of days before us, so we took them to Lillehammer station early one morning to catch the train back to Gardermoen, and we returned two days later.

One very unusual thing that we can see from our window during winter trips, are cars and other vehicles driving on the frozen surface of the lake Losna, which we overlook. Several different tracks seem to be laid out on the snow covered ice, with a lot of bends in them, and we are told that this is organised by the police to train young drivers how to drive on ice covered roads. On one occasion we counted nine cars, one farm tractor and one caravan all in one spot! We asked Ole how thick the ice was, and he replied that it was about 10cm, but that it is resting on the water below which gives it it's strength. Providing that no one opens the sluice at the end of the lake to let water out, all is OK!

During the summer periods we have to tend the garden a bit. There is a small area of grassy

The frozen Losna with the driving course engraved in the snow

52

Wild flowers from our garden

Roadside verges and open areas are covered with wild flowers and strawberries (below), making a carpet of many colours

lawn which has to be cut with a rotary mower which we inherited with the cabin. Unfortunately it has a mind of it's own, and sometimes does not want to start, which it is only asked to once a year! I have now managed to conquer it, but forget how I did it by the next year! The rest of the garden is what is called in Norway "natural". This means it is undulating ground with only natural wild flowers, plants and trees growing on it. There are so many different wild flowers, compared with England, so that in the summer time the garden is a mass of colour like a carpet.

Wild strawberries abound as well, but all of this area, luckily,

The temperamental lawn mower!

needs very little attention, and the weight of the winter snows breaks off the previous year's growth, which starts again when the snow disappears the following spring.

Repainting the roof

In ensuing years we have had several family friends and relations to stay with us during the long hot days of summer, but the summer also is the time to do some work of maintenance to the cabin itself. The floor of the patio needs cleaning and oiling, to help preserve it, and the windows have to have a coat of paint every couple of years. The metal roof also has to be looked after, and that has been repainted black instead of grey, which looks a lot better. We do all of the work ourselves because we enjoy doing it, and all the materials are purchased from the local shops, where we have become quite well known.

The summer of 2006 was soon upon us, and on that trip we were accompanied by my cousin John and his wife Geraldine, who lived about one hours drive from us in England. It was their first visit to Norway, and they were amazed by the high summer temperatures, as they had always thought of Norway as a cold country. This of course is not the case, and we have experienced temperatures there of between -30°C in the winter to +30°C in the summer. We spent the week that they were with us showing them the important places in the area that we had now become accustomed to, like the Maihaugen museum in Lillehammer, Hafjell and Hunderfossen and Aulestad, the home of Bjørnstjerne Bjørnson from 1875-1910. He was a famous Norwegian writer, and the winner of the 1903 Nobel Prize in Literature. In between our tours we would walk the footpaths and sit on walls and contemplate about what a lovely country this was.

"The last of the summer wine"

During the second week of this visit, John and Geraldine went off on a tour of their own around Western Norway, and we met them at Gardermoen on the way back, and all came home together.

Ole had said to us that he was not happy with our flagpole, and said it needed a top or crown on it to make it look right. By the time we got there on the next visit, he appeared with an appropriate top that he had machined on his lathe in his workshop. This was a dome shape with a hole on the underside, to fit on to the top of the pole. The flagpole had been made so that it could be lowered again if necessary, for painting and maintenance, as it had been fixed with two bolts, one upper and one lower. To drop the pole, all that was needed was to remove the bottom bolt and carefully walk backwards and let it swivel on the top one until it would rest on the fence around the patio. The new top was offered up to it, and it fitted perfectly. Whilst down, all was given a fresh coat of paint, and the next day it was erected again. We could now fly the flag properly – but which one?!

The flag of the Devon invaders!

Our flag commandeered by a Viking!

We had brought our own flag over from England, no not the Union Jack, but our very own Devon County flag. After all, this was now our own patch – part of England! The Devon flag is very similar to the flag of Norway, but green in colour, although it has a similar cross in the centre. I told Ole that he would have to produce his passport now every time he came over the small bridge on the way in to the cabin, when the flag was flying, and he gave me a strange look. I think he thought these new "English Vikings" had gone a bit over the top, and might be wanting to invade further! This was not the case of course, as the friendship of the native "Vikings" was far more important to us than anything else.

The Devon flag proved to be most useful on a number of occasions, not least in Lillehammer at the ski jump hill. For several years we attended the World Cup ski jumping competitions there in March of each year, and as everyone else had a flag to wave thought we should have one as well. We tied it to our walking pole and waved it in the air like the others, each time a popular

Our daughter and family at the jump

56

A good party was had by all!

jumper came over the knoll. This caused some consternation with the people beside us, and we kept getting a pat on the shoulder with the question, "Where are you from?", because they didn't recognize the flag. When we told them we were from a county in England, and this was it's flag, they were all very happy, and long conversations took place. On one occasion we were sitting with a bus load from Hamar, and a year later sat beside another bus load from Brummundal. It was a good job that they had come by bus, as I don't think they would have been fit enough to drive home when the jumping had finished!

They came equipped with all the goodies to have a good party, and good party they had, including fancy dress! They included us in their fun and games, and plied us with aquavit, vodka, rum, moose sausage cut off with a pocket knife, and smoked salmon. The friendliness that Norwegian people have to total strangers, has always amazed us. Luckily our car had a SatNav and could find it's own way home!

In Norway, many of the farm animals stray from their seters and roam loose in the forests during the summer period, and it was not uncommon to see them walking on the roads and paths.

Occasionally they would stray into the area around our cabin and had to be enticed out by one means or another – usually a bucket with some cow or sheep nuts in. Lisbeth has had to do this on several occasions, but this is just part of Norwegian daily life in the country areas.

Cows and sheep roam the tracks in the seter areas

But a few cow nuts can work wonders!

Since then anyway, we have had to strengthen our perimeter fence which adjoins the forest behind. We have seen moose nearby, and have been told that brown bears may pass this way sometimes. If you are sitting in your cabin and hear a knock on the door, it is wise to look out of the window first to see who it is, as it might be a hungry bear!

Part of the National Day parade at Tretten 2008

National Day on the 17th May has always been a very important day for the people of Norway, and we have been there on several occasions during the May period. Tretten, our nearest village, always puts on a good show of music and singing.

A young Tretten family in National Dress

We have been to Lillehammer also on the 17th and the procession there is enormous, with many bands playing and students marching. It is customary on National Day for all Norwegians to wear their national costumes, and these are usually very old and have been handed down from one generation to another, and are family heirlooms. They are also extremely finely embroidered and colourful. Sadly we have nothing similar to this in England. It brings a tear to my eye every time I see this, as it is a very patriotic symbol.

NEW YORK 3147   JOHN O'GROATS 874

ISLES OF SCILLY 28
LONGSHIPS LIGHTHOUSE 1½   LILLEHAMMER 1020
9TH JUNE

Terje and Alma at the bottom of England

Gudbrandsdalen. They found it very different in many ways to life at home. We drive on the "wrong" side of the road for a start, and eat very different food to what they were used to, but they joined in the fun, as we did when we visited them. "When in Rome do as Rome does!", is a popular saying in England. We took them to Lands End, the most westerly point of the British Isles, where they had their photograph taken for their holiday pictures.

Not all the traffic during this period has been one way to Norway. In 1997 Terje and Alma came to stay with us in England, and we showed them around our area in Devon, as they had done for us in

In 2008, Ole also came back with us to England for a week. I had told him on the way that he would see more cars in half an hour, than he had seen at Tretten during his lifetime. He really was very shocked to see so many cars on the motorways

60

Ole at Stonehenge

around London, but on the way to our house we stopped off at Stonehenge, a pre historic stone circle, which is a major tourist attraction here. It was somewhere he had always wanted to go.

Ole singing at Vera's 70th birthday party

He came again to us in 2010 to help celebrate Vera's 70th birthday. As he is a member of the Tretten Sangkor, he came prepared to sing two of his local

songs during the party evening, which really impressed the other guests. He is a good singer with a fine voice. In the process of his two weeks with us we showed him how the British used to do battle in the good old days at a mock battle by a group of enthusiasts, took him to Lands End also, as all visitors to our area should go there, and we visited many other places including ancient caves and a nearby castle.

In the summer of 2008 we took another friend of ours called Janet, to the cabin with us. She is a 70 year old from the Bristol area of England, who we had known for many years. You might think at 70 she should be slowing up a little, but not Jan. We took her to all the usual places that other visitors had seen, and she behaved very well. The last place to show her was the Bobsleigh track at Hunderfossen, on our way home one day. Jan was determined to go down the Bob run, despite us saying she was too old for such things. We tried to stop her, but she went off and bought a ticket all the same, telling us that was going to the toilet! The next thing we knew she came back waving the ticket and said, "I'm off!"

Janet after the bob run

She took the truck to the top, and the next thing we saw was her shooting past us at great speed on the wheeled bob. A few minutes later she was sitting quietly with us on a seat having her lunch, as if nothing had happened. You are obviously never too old!

We have always been fascinated by the seasons of the year in Norway, where the summer is hot and the winters are cold. On our many visits to Skeikampen, we have seen it full of caravans half buried in snow in the winter, when the occupants go skiing, and golf being played on the same area in the summer, when we are told that all the caravans have been taken down to the coast for the summer period.

We always say to ourselves that the country has two lives, winter and summer, for which Norwegians are very lucky. At home in England life can be very mundane, and one day is just like another.

It has not all been plain sailing on our visits to Norway. During the winters there is always the potential for water to freeze up, and this happened during the 2010 – 11 winter. This was the first time that this had ever happened in all our years there.

What had happened was that the water pipe from the well had frozen where it crossed under the road, because the weather had been so cold early in the winter before the snow had fallen, and the ground had frozen to a great depth. It is not realized by us in England that the snow, despite being very cold, is also a great insulator, and it is this which normally keeps the minus degrees away from the ground. As it happened, the water had frozen underground in December, and it didn't thaw out until June! This of course causes a few problems – no water in the taps, and no water to flush the toilet. What do we do?

The first thought is to melt some snow on the stove, which we tried, but unless you have done this, you don't realize that a

saucepan full of snow only produces about 2cm of water in the pan when melted – not much good for flushing! Luckily Ole and Lisbeth's water supply was still OK, so we lived for a week on churns of water which had to be hauled up from the house. A little inconvenient for everyone, but it saved our bacon. To combat this happening again, we have now had to insert a special warming cable inside the water pipe, which hopefully will stop it happening again, but we will have to wait and see!

A couple of years before there had been another incident at the well, as when we arrived no water seemed to be coming down the pipe to the taps. I borrowed Ole's snow shoes to cross over the deep snow to try to find the well, which was buried under a metre of the white stuff. It was lucky that I knew roughly where it was, and after prodding with a long stick I found it. I thought it might have been frozen there, and had to have a look inside, but it was too dark as it was late evening. I went back for a shovel and traversed the snow again and

Man with a mission!

started digging to get at the heavy concrete cover which was on top of the well. Unless you have had to do this you do not realize what a hard job it is. It is difficult to stand anyway, and as soon as you use the shovel to lift something you start sinking further in. You also have to clear a hole twice as large as the well to be able to lift the cover off. Luckily this time the water wasn't frozen, but the filter on

the end of the pipe had blocked, and that was why we didn't have any water in the cabin. The filter was cleaned and all was well, and all the snow I had just dug out had to be put back in the hole again to act as insulation!

If you are not acquainted with Norwegian cabins, you probably do not realize that they "move" in conjunction with the state of the surrounding ground. You can go on a visit in the summer and all the doors and windows will open and shut OK, but go back again at another time, or in the winter, and everything seems to stick a bit. We have now got used to this, and have got a resident wood plane in our tool cupboard, which is most useful at times. None of it is drastic, but it does move!

Probably our worst experience was when we took a four day trip further north, and away from the cabin, to stay at a hotel in Geiranger for a few nights.

We had taken the car down the fjord on the ferry to Hellesylt, with the intention of driving back over the high ground of

Geiranger - one of Norways most beautiful areas

Strynfjellet, to see some summer snow and skiing. This is where the ski athletes practice in the summer time. This was something like a 150km round trip. All went well, we saw the snow and the skiers, and proceeded on to get back to our hotel in Geiranger for supper time. We needed to stop to fill the car up with diesel at the very small filling station there, which was a bit crowded, and the front wheel of the car accidently just caught the concrete base of the pump. A hissing noise was heard, and when we looked the tyre was flat, and on inspection actually split! Thinking I could change the wheel to put on the

spare one, on looking in the back found that there was no spare.

This I could not believe! We were only 2km from the hotel, but eventually had to go 120km to get there! It was 5pm on a Saturday evening, the worst time to have any sort of problem. There was no tyre supplier in the village, so I phoned the hire company's rescue service. The nearest rescue lorry was 100km away, and he was already out on another job – we would have to wait. We waited and waited for three hours, and eventually help arrived. "Can't do anything here" said the driver, "you will have to come with me", so we were loaded up on his lorry and taken back to his workplace at Stryn, where a new tyre could be fitted. We were both squeezed in to the cab with the driver, and were taken at high speed through many tunnels and around many bends to arrive at Stryn about an hour later. The driver luckily was very jovial, and he gave us a commentary on the countryside that we were passing through all the way back, and we told him about our life in England. The tyre was fixed, but we still had to drive ourselves the 100km back to Geiranger, a journey we had already done in the afternoon, where we unfortunately were too late for our supper!

It was what we call "a bad day all round", but luckily we haven't had too many of those! The following day we headed to Trollstigen and descended the very steep and winding roads on the way back "home" to the cabin.

The sad end of a long day!

After that things seemed to get better, and we took a trip to see our long time original friend Liv and her husband Erik, at their cabin in Gålå, about one hours drive further up the road. We had done this trip many times before, and we always looked forward to our annual get together. Liv also has a Dachshund called Donna, and the two ladies always liked to talk about Dachshund things. Erik was like me, a practical person who always liked to be doing something outside the cabin when the weather was good, and as Liv said earlier, "If you have a cabin there is always something to do!"

The view from our cabin is tremendous on days with good weather, as it is high above the lake. On days of bad weather, we have found ourselves living above the clouds, sometimes for many days at a time. We have also seen small aircraft flying below us, but we have now got

Life above the clouds!

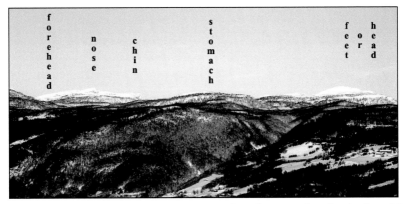

f					s			f	h
o		n	c		t			e	e
r		o	h		o			e	a
e		s	i		m			r	d
h		e	n		a			t	
e					c				
a					h				
d									

The "Old Men mountain" - can you see it? - there is a head at both ends!

used to this and take it all for granted. If you look across the lake on a good day you can see a mountain ridge the other side in the distance. This we have named "The old men mountain", as to us it resembles two old men lying down asleep. To us it seems quite lifelike, and I can quite see where the mystical Troll's came from, although

they can be seen better in the winter when the trees are heavy with snow.

There is also a small valley cut into the hillside opposite, which we call "The cloud factory". In certain temperatures new clouds seem to be produced from this small area in large quantities, and float up into the sky and generally stay at one level. They are all shapes and sizes. All of a sudden production will stop, and you may not see any more for days. One very important cloud produced from here was "Cloud 9", where everyone wants to be of course, and we were lucky enough to have been able to capture it in a picture!

Cloud 9!

68

The cabin looks down on the E6 road about 2km away, and it is a road that is well used everyday by large lorries towing trailers taking provisions up to the north of the country. At the weekends it is even more busy with cars, as most Norwegians seem to have a cabin in the mountains, and they all like to take a short break from Friday to Sunday evening. On Friday's we watch them all going north, nose to tail, and on Sunday evening see them all going south again back to their homes. We always say that how nice it is to sit here, and watch the world go by, and not have to be part of it!

Beside the cabin there is a very high section of rock, which is covered in trees. On the top of this there is one single tree which stands out from the others, and I call it "The Lone Tree". If you know where to look, it can be seen from a long way away, as you drive up the E6. The climb to it through the forest is steep and hard going at times, and one of our standard comments to any guests we

have, is that if they get to it they will be awarded our "Lone Tree Medal". Not many have taken up the challenge, and so far Vera and I are the only ones to have made it to the top, so we have awarded a medal to each other!

The lone tree towers above the rest

During the fifty years that we have been involved with Norway, we have seen many changes. Not just the moving of the airport from Fornebu to Gardermoen, which was good for us, but more recently the E6 up from Oslo has changed out of all recognition. It is no longer a narrow and slow road, as much of it has been made up to dual carriageway so we can drive a little faster. This appears to be an ongoing project for some years to come. Having been able to observe the progress of this, we have been amazed by what is involved in roadmaking here compared with in England. At home rarely do road constructors come across rock, but in Norway it seems to be 75% or more of the whole distance. All of this has to be drilled, explosives inserted, and the rock blasted apart before they can even get going. The new tunnel currently being constructed between Øyer and Tretten, which is 4.5km long, is a testament to Norwegian engineering. Over the years we have found that if Norwegians want to get from one place to another, and there is a mountain in the way, they do not go up and over, they just go straight through! There are some very impressive tunnels in Western Norway, up to 20 km in length, and one we went through was like a corkscrew where you started off at the bottom and went around in circles until you came out at the top. How this was calculated is beyond me! If they want to get to an offshore island, more than likely they will drill under the sea instead of building a bridge, as they have now done to Nordkapp, where we had to cross the last bit by ferry when we went there in 1998.

The new Tretten tunnel being built

The last frontier - Svalbard

Considering ourselves now to be half Norwegian, there was one part of the country that we had never visited. This was of course one of the remotest places on Earth - Svalbard. It was a long way from our cabin, but for my 70th birthday I had made up my mind that it was now or never to visit this place which was only 1309 km from the North Pole. Probably many Norwegians have never been there either, but I was determined to do it before the end.

We set off from our home in England on 17th March 2012 on a voyage of discovery, flying from London to Tromsø, where we spent the night. The following day we flew on again to Longyearbyen the capital and only real town on Svalbard. We were blessed with a fine day for our flight, and were able to see everything on the way in. We had been talking to a Norwegian lady on the plane who had been there, and her description of it was "it is somewhere else!"

That certainly proved to be true. On landing at Longyearbyen we were immediately made aware of how remote a place it was and what the dangers were.

The approach to Svalbard showing the sea ice

The "somewhere else" comment by the lady had however become very apparent as we approached the islands, and could see all the ice jutting out into the sea from the land mass. Of course what we saw was only a tiny piece of the whole area of Svalbard itself, which is massive and barren like the moon. To want to live there you need to be a special type of person. Apart from the 1800 residents, there is a large contingent of scientific people.

The first day we took a walk around the town to get ourselves orientated, before making some arrangements to do some more exciting things. The town of Longyearbyen is a very basic place compared with other towns in Norway, and everything has to be shipped in for the residents to live there. There are no trees on the islands and no farms to produce food, although the town is well heated by a communal system which pipes hot water to the houses.

On day two we booked up for a four hour guided snow scooter trip out into the more remote valleys, and had to be kitted out in very heavy and stiff thermal suits, with thick gloves, boots and helmets. We could hardly walk, but they were very necessary to keep us warm.

Eventually, after being given some instructions on how to drive the snow scooter, we set off in convoy and followed our guide for 20 km. Two old pensioners from England having a day out - wow!

All togged up and ready to go!

On day three we had booked for a dog sledding trip in the early evening. We were picked up from the hotel by our guide, and placed in the back of her truck for the 10km journey to the place where we once again had to get kitted out in the now well known thermal suits, boots and gloves. It was a bit easier this time as we knew what to do. Then we were taken to the starting point and kennels where we had to harness up the dogs, before starting our journey into the unknown. This was a tremendous experience and another 20 km was covered. At the end we were invited to handle the new puppies, to help to socialise them.

Sadly now, our adventure to Svalbard was coming to an end, and the next day we had to return to Oslo via Tromsø. As we arrived late in the evening we stayed there for the night. On the next day, we were going to do something we had not done together since OL in 1994.

Reunion with old friends

O n the way up to Tretten from Gardermoen, we had arranged to stop off at Hamar to see Ragnhild Hanum. We had not seen her together for 18 years, although I had seen her myself about 8 years ago. We wondered what she would be like after all this time, as she was now 93 years old.

Ragnhild in 1968

Ragnhild, and her husband Anders, were if you remember, the Norwegian family that first contacted us in 1961. She was then about 43.

The years have passed for all of us since then, but we are still here! We have always kept in contact at Christmas, but were looking forward to meeting her again.

Ragnhild in 2012

She still has a lovely smile on her face, and still lives on the same farm where we first met her. She was really pleased to see us, as we were her. Our memories of the times that we have stayed there, will remain with us for ever.

On the following day we had also arranged to meet someone else, who we had not seen for 46 years! This was Berit Huuse, (in the yellow jacket), who was one of the girls who stayed with us in 1966. Now of course she has been married for many years and has children and grandchildren of her own.

Liv and Berit had always remained good friends since those early days, and we had a good few hours getting up to date with what had happened to all of us during the 46 year gap in our lives.

This meeting together of all of us, strengthened our resolve to meet again on a more regular basis in the future, so that this long "journey" which had taken up a major part of all our lives might continue until the end. It is even possible that these two Norwegian girls may retrace their footsteps to England and have their photographs taken in the same place again after all this time!

The "Four Musketeers", Liv, Roger, Vera and Berit

The "Fifth Musketeer" from the original 1966 picture, (page 13), the baby, can no longer be included in the picture above. He has now grown a little, and so has his family. He, on the right, is seen here with his wife and three boys plus his mother at Skeikampen.

And finally!

When this story started in 1961, I was 20 years old, as were the others involved. Unfortunately I am no longer that, and have now passed the "maximum" Norwegian age of 39, and am still alive! It doesn't take much mathematics to work out that if you add 50 to 20 you get 70, and I am still alive here as well - indeed we both are! We have now been married for 48 of our 50 Norwegian years, and hope to get to 50 with that also. Perhaps the book should have been called "50 – 50"!

It took us a little time to get used to being entertained by the families that we visited. In England when we are eating a meal, we usually only have three courses of food, a starter or soup, a main course, and a pudding, and one helping of each. We soon found out that in Norway things were done differently, and that the main course would be offered several times before moving on to the pudding. In the early days we would take what we thought would be enough for us, to find out that we were still expected to eat more and more. We therefore soon learnt not to take too much the first time! If you have never tasted a Norwegian salmon, caught in a nearby lake by a Norwegian man, and cooked by a Norwegian woman, you have not lived. Such a taste you will not find anywhere else, and is something to die for. I can still taste the first salmon I had fifty years ago!

The timber houses of the country have always intrigued us by their superb design and internal layouts, many of which still contain classic furniture which has been handed down through the generations. It is not just the important museum houses that have such furniture, as it can be seen equally in many an ordinary domestic property.

Throughout this period we have been amazed by the friendliness of the Norwegian people in general, and particularly those we have been closely involved with, and we would like to thank them all for that. Their help and guidance throughout our long journey has always been most welcome and useful.

The "Journey to Paradise", as I said in the beginning, was the result of a chance encounter by two people who didn't know each other, and had this not happened I would not be here to tell the story. They could have just passed by each other on the ferry without speaking, but they didn't, and from that first conversation a friendship was sparked which has lasted half a century.

It is interesting to record here that this story now goes full circle, and that the young Norwegian girl on the ferry, Anne Helene Hanum, is still alive and the same age as me. She has now volunteered to check my Norwegian translation so that the book can be published in Norway as well as in England. This to me is a wonderful gesture of friendship, for which I give her my heartfelt thanks.

Here we are, sat outside the same cabin at Sjusjøen in 2009, as I was in 1963, (see page 10), with Olav and Anne Helene on the right soaking up the sun

I like to think that throughout this last half century, all those involved in "Team Paradise" have worked together for the benefit of English – Norwegian co-operation, and a better understanding between the two countries. There have been reciprocal journeys, and a lot has been learnt by both sides about each others cultures and customs. This has all been done on a private basis, and not through any official Anglo - Norsk organisation, and the results have been outstanding.

Our Norwegian friends have often said to us "Why Tretten?"

The word Tretten, to those who are not aware, is the Norwegian word for thirteen, (13) in English. Thirteen is not classed as a lucky number in England, but we also have a saying here which is "Thirteen – lucky for some". No need to say any more really!

So the flag flies on for a little longer – God willing!

The "Little House on the Prairie" , (Paradise!), with Tretten in the valley below

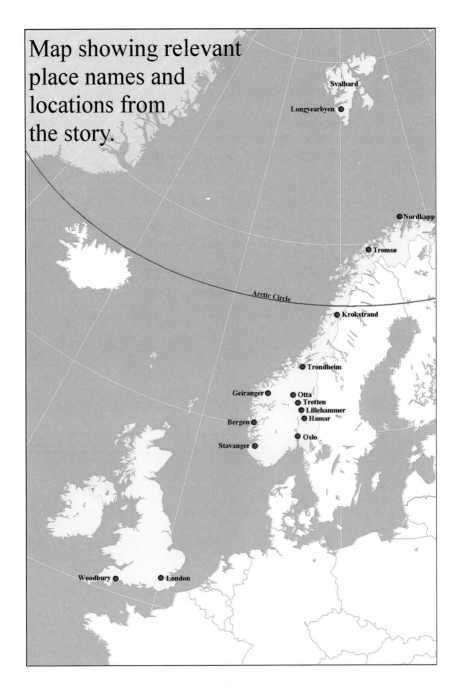

Map showing relevant place names and locations from the story.